HOPE IS A SALESPERSON'S CURRENCY

©JOHN SCHAFER

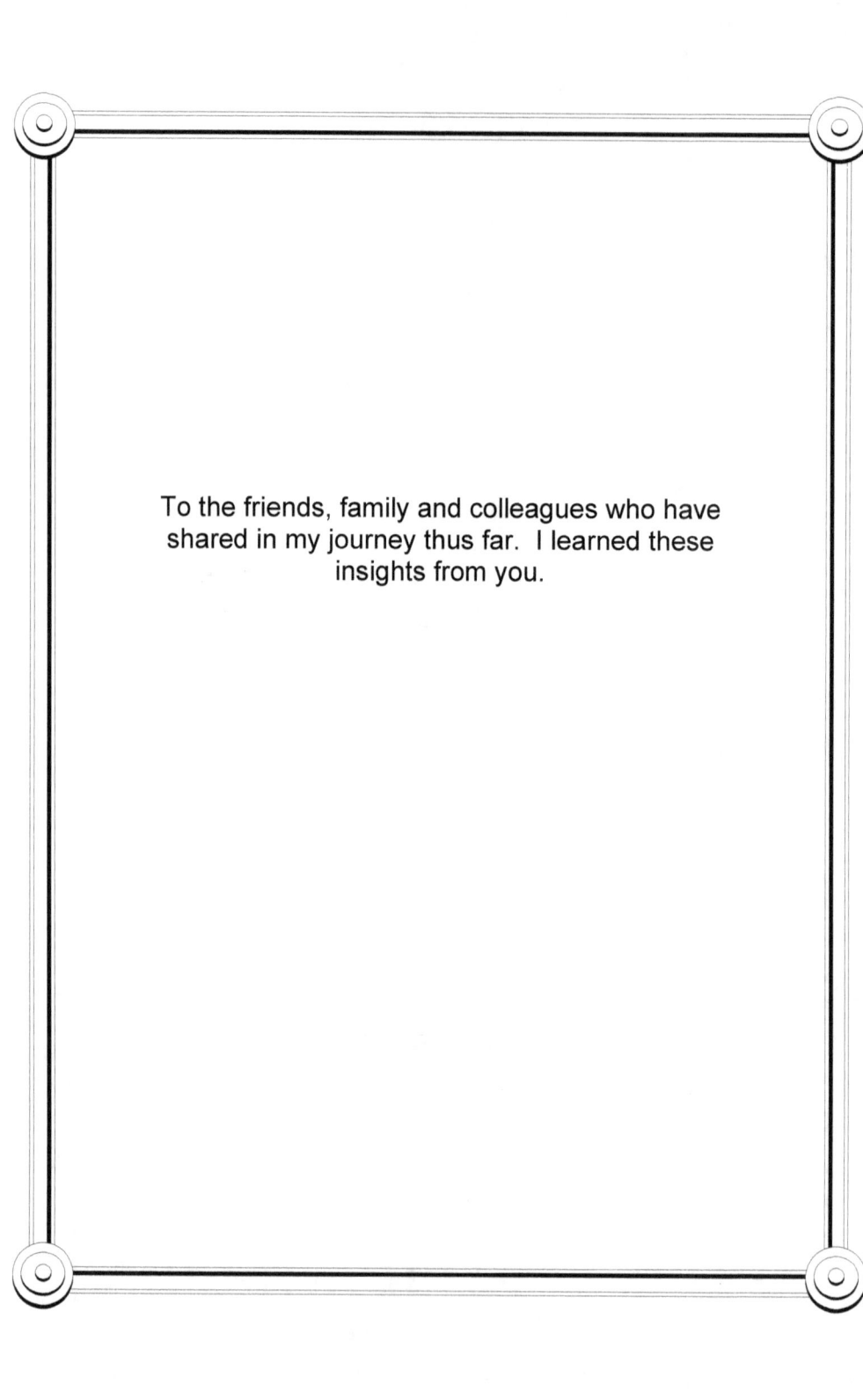

To the friends, family and colleagues who have shared in my journey thus far. I learned these insights from you.

INTRODUCTION

I have been a groom, a busboy, a telephone operator, a dishwasher, a sales clerk, a land surveyor, an engineering technician, a restaurant manager, an automotive shop manager, a telemarketer, a temp for a firm computerizing Child Support Records, a sales rep, and a sales manager.

Nearly 25 years ago I started my first outside sales position. I was green, possessed what I thought was raw talent and was eager to succeed. I completed my company's sales training courses. They were of little help. I still made all the mistakes new sales people make. Since those early days, I have spent the rest of my career as a student of sales, determined to improve my skills. I have listened to tapes, read books, attended seminars, participated in numerous company sponsored sales trainings, picked the brains of the reps I considered Sales Masters, learned from the reps I managed and slowly learned from my own mistakes.

It is my hope that the snippets of insight contained in this book will help those new to the profession as well as the veterans of the craft.

Good Selling.

Hope is a sales person's currency.

I don't mean, "I hope for the sale". Or, "I hope the customer understood my presentation". What I mean is sales people deal in possibilities: the hope for the crack in the door that has been closed innumerable times before; the hope that the prospect understands your solution; the simple expectation of success. It's what keeps us knocking on those next 100 doors knowing they may be shut on us abruptly as well. We knock on that next door because we have hope. It takes dedication, hard work, and resilience. You have to trust in your abilities. You have to believe in your product, your company and yourself. You have to *expect* a positive outcome. You have to be confident. This is a key foundation for your success. You must have a belief in the certainty of your success. Many of us fear our own success and consign ourselves to the ranks of the mediocre. You need to be open to the certainty of your success.

It is a hope built upon a solid foundation of effort. A confident expectation brought about by sweat and preparation.

It's not a sale until the customer pays the bill.

Obvious? Perhaps, but, how many times have you assumed the customer would buy and they didn't? Or, they placed their order and returned it. Or, they never paid their bill. I've claimed my share of prospects as wins that never materialized. Don't succumb to the temptation. You will have instances where you *know* you have the sale but you don't get it. Don't claim credit until the bill is paid. Sometimes in the giddiness of getting a verbal commitment, we lose sight of what a sale really is. By all means, if you get a verbal commitment, get excited; just remember the customer has to pay the invoice before the sale is complete.

An order is not a sale. A purchase is a sale.

Go find 20 prospects that tell you no.

Your success, in large part, is decided by how long that takes.

I followed this adage early in my career. I would choose a section of my territory and knock on doors. I would come home and recount all the people who said no to me. Learn to celebrate the rejections, knowing you are that much closer to success. Most prospects will tell you they are not interested. Until you get proficient at uncovering unmet needs, all of them will.

Sales *is* a numbers game. Be the rep that gets 20 no's in day versus the rep that takes a week. Do not forget, however, to continue to call back on those who did tell you no.

Sometimes you have to call on the same prospect 20 times. Don't assume once is enough.

Remember to always be looking for your next customer.

It doesn't matter what you think.

You might think you have the best product or service, *ever*. You can't wait to tell everybody all about it. Stop yourself. Find out what your prospects problems, concerns or aspirations are. Let them talk more than you do. Then you'll know if what you have is what they need.

This also applies to your current customers as well. You may think they are loyal. Ask them. Make sure they are not considering your competition. Make sure they are happy with your products or services. Don't get surprised by the loss of what you thought was a never-will-leave-me customer. Never assume that your long term customers aren't looking at the competition. I have found many customers after years of buying from me couldn't help themselves and talked to and often bought from my competitors. It was almost as if they thought they were missing out on something; or, were somehow obligated to buy from someone else.

No news is not good news. **No news is no news**. Why have you stopped communicating with your current customers? Why are you allowing your competition the ability to come in and take your business?

Sales people are often opinionated. Ask your customers what their opinions are; don't offer yours.

You want a raise? Go sell something. You determine your income.

I love being in sales. My paycheck is never the same. I can't imagine receiving the same pay every paycheck. You, the sales professional, have the ability to affect your income. How fortunate you are. You do not have to wait for a cost of living increase or an annual merit raise. You can go get a raise today. In the nearly 25 years I have been in outside sales and sales management, my income has gone up every year but one. Go sell something. Earn yourself an immediate raise. It's what your company is expecting you to do.

You have one of the few jobs where what you do can affect your income. A clerk doesn't have that. An administrator doesn't have that. You have the ability to increase your income with your actions. How wonderfully exciting.

You will be rewarded for your successes. Now go sell something.

Why didn't you get the sale?

Every sale you do not get is because you missed something. You did not ask enough questions. You did not ask the right questions.

Never assume anything. You do not know what is going on behind the scenes. Sometimes, you need to rely on more than one person to uncover the untold story. It is okay to conduct a post-sale meeting with your prospects to discuss why you did not get the sale. I do this regularly and use that information to guide me on my next sale. Every sales process should teach you something, whether you land the account or not.

Often times you'll find it was an unmet need you didn't uncover. Or a relationship you didn't know about. Or a change agent you were unaware of.

Learn from every lost opportunity. Apply that knowledge to the next one.

Never send an email that couldn't be published on the front page of your newspaper.

It took me a while to learn this. I fired off many an email early in my career I wish I could have recalled. There are some that even make me wince when I think about them. Once you send an email, it is out there to be potentially forwarded to anyone. I consider this every time I compose an email. You should too.

Imagine your emails are printed on your company's letterhead. Read them before you send them. Often, I edit my original composition. Sometimes, simply taking a pause is enough for you to reconsider.

I also believe we have become too reliant on emails. We send emails to the people in the cubicle next to us. Get up and go talk to them. Or call them. What sense does it make to send dozens of emails back and forth when a 30-second phone call would end the confusion? Emails are easily misinterpreted. And their tone is always more negative than you intended.

Also, don't cc the world. The more people you cc the greater the chance that no one will address the issue. They all think someone else will. If you want something done – send the request to one person. If you must send an email to multiple recipients, clearly identify what you wish each of them to do.

If you are angry or frustrated allow yourself a
moment to collect yourself before sending an email.

If you don't know; say you don't know—and offer to find out.
If you made a mistake; admit you made a mistake—and offer a solution.

Some salespeople have given our profession the reputation that we are nothing more than a bunch of liars, thieves, and snakes. Do not become one these sales reps. If you don't know the answer—don't make something up—find out and inform your customer. Customers do not expect you to have all the answers, but they do expect you to be honest with them.

Early in my career, I forgot to place a critical order for one of my customers. The purchasing manager was berating me about why he didn't have his product. I calmly informed him that I had made a mistake, forgot to order it, but that I had the product on the way. He knew I was new and he paused, looked me in the eye and said, "It takes a big man to admit he made a mistake. You will do well." I have never forgotten that life lesson.

Honesty can have a positive outcome. Dishonesty will always haunt you.

An upfront and honest salesperson will always have loyal, long-term customers.

I don't like "Win – Win – Win."

I do like "Give – Give – Give." I give a little, the customer gives a little, and my company gives a little.

To me, sales is not a sports game. I am not trying to beat my customer. I am trying to solve an issue for my customer. And, the concept that we can all win strikes me as disingenuous.

Many times reps and their companies lose because of the desire to *win* the account. What are you winning? Is it your pride that leads you to make a bad deal for your company? Or do you make a bad deal for the customer because of your arrogance?

Let's enter the realm of true sales professionals and negotiate an agreement that works for all parties. This will involve some give and take. If your prospect asks for a lower price; ask for something in return. The race to landing the account at all costs is not an event you want to "win".

Why do your customers buy from you?

Have you ever asked yourself that question? Better yet, have you ever asked any of your customers that question? Why not? You not ask your prospects why they buy from their current supplier, wouldn't it be good to know why your current customers buy from you? You could put that information to good use. You might uncover some things you need to change. You might find out some reasons you'd never considered. You also might find a customer willing to promote your product or service for you.

Your customers should want to buy from you. Find out why they do. Use that information.

Attitude is the great equalizer.

I will take attitude over skills, experience, and charisma – every time. A good attitude is essential to your success. If you find yourself bemoaning your situation, stop. Do something about it. Make a plan. Do something different. Read a business book; listen to a motivational speaker. Get yourself out of the rut you are in. Find your passion.

Businesses reward employees with good attitudes. Sales come to reps with good attitudes. Promotions come to people with good attitudes. You're in sales; you should have a good attitude. You alone control your attitude, and because of that, you control your success.

Positive behavior yields positive results. Every time.

Would you buy from yourself?

I often use this as a barometer for the sales people I meet: "Would I buy from them?" You need to ask *yourself* that question – would you buy from yourself? Seriously? Would you buy from you? Do you project an air of honesty, integrity, and competence? Are you punctual and courteous? Do you convey an aura of professionalism? We've all meet these types of reps – are you one? Commit to improving your craft each day. Be one of those reps that everyone would buy from. Picture in your mind an ideal sales rep and emulate that behavior.

Subscribe to newsletters. Read books. Listen to audio tapes. Take all the training your can - even the most mundane can teach you something.

Balance is key to a happy life.

The biggest trap to the sales profession that I see is that you are never done.

There is *always* another call to make, another product to quote, another proposal to present. It can become all-consuming. You can only work 14 hour days for so long. You will lose your edge and your attitude. It is important to set time aside for just you. Turn off your phone. Do not check your email or voice mail. Relax and recharge. Use your vacation days. You've earned them; use them. You will be happier and more productive. Find something outside of work to engage your free time. Whether you take up a hobby or a sport or a cause, you need to have something other than work you are passionate about.

You need a balanced work/home life to be happy and successful.

You don't want every customer.

You may think you do. You don't.

Your sales manager may cringe at this concept.
That's their job – to motivate you to go after every
sale. Your job is to realize you do not want them
all. Some of them should be buying from your
competitors. Look through your book of business
and identify those customers that take up the
majority of your time. My guess is that these are
the customers that make your company the least
amount of profit and you the least amount of
commission. Consider severing your relationship
or at the very least altering your relationship. It is
okay to terminate your association with any client.
You want clients that value what you and your
company offer. The more customers you have like
that, the more successful you will be.

Sometimes the sales process includes finding out
you don't want to do business with each other.

It is the customer's money you are spending.

We have all been counselled to spend the company's money as if it were our own. But it really isn't our money - that money came from our customers, who purchased the products or services offered by our company.

Companies exist because of the money collected from their customers.

Your paycheck contains your customer's money. Your expenses are reimbursed with customer money. Have we lost sight of that?

Is your customers' money being put to good use? Would you want your customers to know how you're spending their money?

If you didn't get the sale, don't blame the prospect. Blame yourself.

I call it: "The story you didn't learn." Every lost sale can be attributed to you, the sales person, not discovering a critical piece of information. *Every one.* If you lost on price, you did not uncover what is valuable to the customer so they chose price. If you lost because the incumbent has always had the business, you did not find what a compelling reason to change would be for them. Think back on every lost sale you've had. *It's your fault.* No one else to blame but you. Now there is a positive to this fact. You can work to uncover the hidden information you will need to close the sale. You control your success. What a wonderful profession we're in.

Are you talking to the right person?

All of us were taught this in every sales class we've ever taken. Do you subscribe to it? Is your decision maker really the decision maker? I've lost accounts because I thought I had an iron clad relationship with the right person, only to learn someone else was in control. Is your sales process delayed because you are not talking to the right person? Don't always take their word for it. Most people are averse to telling you they really do not have the authority needed. Dig around in the account. You might be talking to an influencer. You need to talk to the decision maker.

Does everyone know your name?

I am always impressed upon entering an account when the receptionist, the accounting department, marketing and operations all know who their rep is. This rep has taken ownership of his business and is not giving his competition an opportunity to make a run at his account. The more people you know within an account the more opportunities you are presented with for uncovering unknown sales. They know who you are and what you sell and will seek you out to buy from you. Imagine that, customers seeking *you* out. Now that's a sales professional.

Know when to walk away.

Sales people want to win the account. Often at all costs. Every request for proposal does not warrant a response. If you can't make money, walk away. If you can't meet your customer's needs, walk away. If your product is not a good fit, walk away. You need to know where the line is for you and be prepared to exit. Know this for every prospect and every customer. Have a firm line that you will not cross. Your job is to make your company money. If the deal doesn't do that; don't do the deal.

I have seen too many accepted proposals that were "foot in the door" losers that stayed losers and never went past the getting-to-know-you stage. Why should you sacrifice your profit margin with no assurance of more business to come? Poor salesmanship. It's easy (and lazy) to drop your price to entice a customer; however, once you head down that path the ability to overcome the inertia of low price is next to impossible. If you've done that you've simply let your customer know that price is all you have to offer.

**Confidence in yourself, your product and
your company is essential for sales success.**

Do you portray yourself, your product and your
company with the confidence it deems?
Confidence comes from knowledge. Have you
studied your product? Have you learned about
your customer's business? Have you practiced
your craft? Have you prepared yourself?
Confidence is preparation. How do you prepare for
each day, each call, each year? Are you engaged
in learning? Preparation will give you confidence
which will give you success.

Just as a great actor rehearses his lines and a
great musician spends hours honing his skills; you
should too. Confidence comes from ability. Ability
comes from training. Have you committed yourself
to continuous improvement? Do you invest in
yourself? Do you have the discipline to work on
improving yourself?

The customer is not always right.

The customer is *not* always right. I can't believe we teach that they are. What we are really saying is: we won't acknowledge any customer errors. We won't hold customers accountable. Or, we'll pretend the customer is always right and then create policies our front line people have to enforce that say otherwise.

Let's acknowledge that customers will make mistakes. They will place late orders and expect next day delivery. They will exceed their credit limit and still expect you to process their order. They will have past due invoices and expect you to ignore them.

How you handle your errant customers will determine your long-term relationship with them, and your long-term success as a salesperson. Allowing a customer to place a late order due to unforeseen circumstances is great customer relationship building. Allowing that same customer to place the majority of their orders late for next day delivery is not. That is allowing a company policy to be consistently broken for no good reason. This customer knows he has you in a subservient role and will continue to take advantage of his authority over you. This is not how partnerships are built. Consultative selling does not work in an imbalanced relationship.

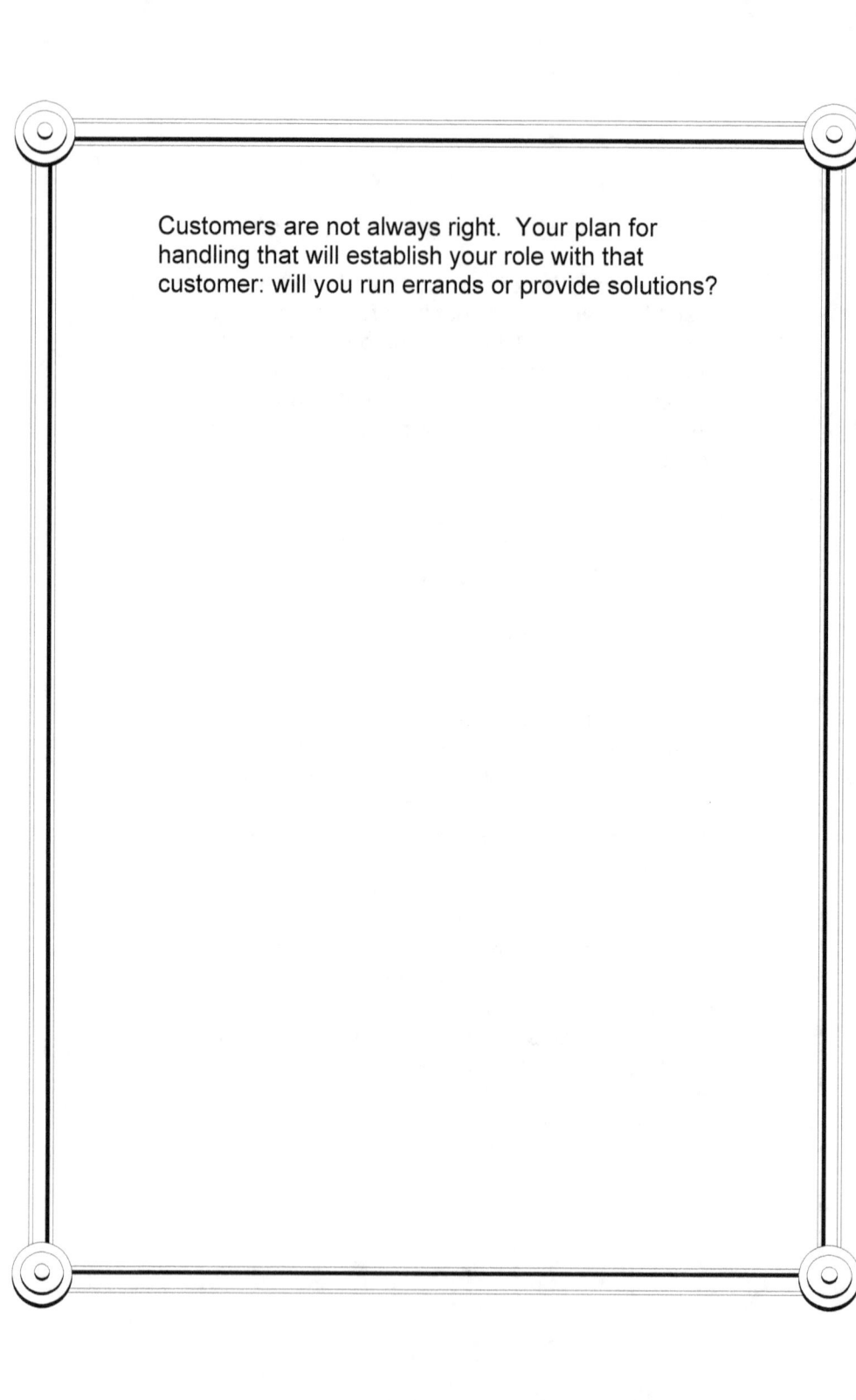

Customers are not always right. Your plan for
handling that will establish your role with that
customer: will you run errands or provide solutions?

Treat all you meet with respect.

I started my career selling institutional cleaning products to the hospitality industry. My end users were dishwashers and housekeepers. They used my products but did not make the decision to buy them. However, they could influence that decision or sabotage my efforts. I learned early on to treat everyone with respect. Do not rebuke the receptionist who will not let you see your prospect. She is doing her job as a gatekeeper. She also can inform the prospect of your disrespectful behavior, thus costing you any chance of landing the sale. People get promoted. Dishwasher today; Food and Beverage Manager tomorrow.

Excessive profits are always short term.

The business community is littered with the remnants of companies who went too far.

Remember the dot com bust?

Enron?

The housing bubble?

All in search of excessive and often obscene profits.

Do not fall into this same trap. Do not charge a naïve customer an exorbitant price because you can – someone, someday will point out your overcharging and you will lose the account and your credibility. A long term customer is always preferable and a fair profit makes that more likely.

Laugh at yourself.

Why wouldn't you?

Don't allow yourself to lose your sense of humor. We've all dealt with the stuffed shirt who is so serious it's painful. Humor is a great liberator. A well-timed turn of phrase can clear the way for progress. It is also a great way to relieve stress. Laughing at yourself is good for your soul. It brightens people's days. No one likes someone so serious they cannot see any humor in themselves.

Don't forget the human element to selling.

Become an expert.

As a sales rep, you represent an industry; your company provides products and services that support that industry and you call on businesses within that industry. The more you know about that industry – trends, challenges, competitors, best practices – the better you can position your company's products and services to solve those issues. You will be much more successful positioning yourself as an expert in your field.

If you've thought through how your company's products and services solve your customer's challenges you'll be perceived as an advisor rather than someone simply pushing product. Don't stop at the features and benefits your products have; think how the benefits of your products solve a customer issue.

Challenge yourself to learn something each day.

It could be a new word. It could be something about your customer's business. It could be a feature of one of your products. I subscribe to numerous e-newsletters and industry magazines. I dedicate time each day to read them.

Learn something new today. It will help you on your path to success.

Embrace your curiosity.

Set goals. Write them down. Track your progress. You'll be amazed at what you accomplish.

I start each year with 3-6 goals (any more is mostly unmanageable). I write them down. I plan how I am going to achieve them and I track my progress. Do I always achieve all of them? No. But I do achieve more than if I had not set them and worked towards meeting them. A goal, not written down and planned for, is no more than a dream. Dreams may occupy our thoughts; they do nothing to help us achieve success.

Plan your time or someone else will. Their plan for you will help them; not you.

Take control of your success by working towards achieving *your* goals.

Learn as much from your bad bosses as you learn from your good ones.

We've all had horrid bosses. They can still teach us something – even if it's what not to do. Or they may possess a quality, like determination, you had not considered.

I had a boss once with all the charm and personality of a ream of paper; yet, he taught me that perseverance can overcome a lack of charisma. What he lacked in personality he more than made up for in hard work. He taught me to use the gifts I have been given rather than yearning for those I did not possess.

Everyone can teach us something. Be open to discovering what.

Always carry a pen.

A pen should be an integral part of your wardrobe.
Do not leave the house without one. It is a tool to
be carried by every sales professional. How can
you take notes or write down an order without one?

A carpenter needs a hammer; a mechanic needs a
wrench; a fisherman needs a net. You, as a sales
professional, need a pen.

Customers buy from people they like.

Be agreeable and friendly. Be polite and respectful. Remember, it is about the customer, not you. Research them and their company. The internet is a treasure trove of information – don't just look around their office and notice their personal items and think that's all you have to do to build rapport. Practice the art of small talk – but go beyond discussing their nick nacks. Always be neutral when it comes to politics and religion. Engage them in talking about themselves.

Persistence is nearly as important as attitude for sales success.

I once called on the same prospect for three years before I got the sale. Three years. Our normal selling cycle was 6-9 months. Three years of consistently knocking on his door. Three years of being rejected.

The successful sales reps persevere and know that much about the sales process is timing. If you do not consistently call on your prospects you stand a good chance of not being there when the time is right. If I had given up, even after two years, I would not have landed the account. Every no gets you closer to a yes.

Persistence can make up for a lack of charisma, skills, and experience, just as attitude can.

Most salespeople talk too much.

This is a concern for many of us. We are people people and love to talk. Stop. Save your gabbing for your friends, family and co-workers. Your prospects should be talking more than you. If that's not the case, reevaluate yourself. Ask questions and wait for the answer. Take a deep breath before you speak, which gives the customer time to talk. Do not feel like you have to fill in every moment of silence. Silence can be good for the sales process. Prospects need time to consider your offer. They can't do that if you're talking.

Practice the art of listening. Don't lose a sale because *you* talked too much.

Look around your customers account. Be observant. You never know what you might uncover.

Imagine never making another cold call in your career. You could accomplish this by simply focusing on your existing customers and selling them everything your company offers. When I sold institutional chemicals I would write down everything each customer was buying from me and everything they could buy from me. Each call I would work to get another product into my existing accounts. You already have the relationship established, utilize it.

As a Sales Manager, I often told my reps that they would never have to sell another new account if they simply sold everything they could to their existing customers.

Quotas will never go away.

Companies require growth to survive. Quotas are their way to ensure this growth. Do you have a plan for yours? Have you identified your top prospects and created a plan for each? Have you given consideration to penetrating your existing account base? Have you committed yourself to learning something new about the products your company offers? Or are you going to wing it? Or perhaps complain that your quota isn't fair? Have you thought of a creative way you might market your company, your product or yourself? What is your plan to compensate for the 10% loss of your existing sales that will occur due to attrition?

Be truthful.

Obvious. Often times forgot. Don't spin the truth.
Don't parse your words. Also, always tell your boss
the bad news yourself. Do not let him find out from
someone else. Don't tell some story to your
customers about why their order isn't showing up
today. Tell them the truth; offer them a solution;
figure out a way to prevent it from happening again
and follow up.

Make your sales presentation a conversation.

This took me the longest to learn. I thought your sales presentation had to be given the way they trained you. I drove myself crazy for years trying to remember all the proper steps from the latest sales training class. It is a wonder I ever sold anything. Have a conversation with your prospect. Don't throw up features and benefits because that's what you think you should do. Don't try to navigate through some predetermined course of events. Research their company. Ask questions. Listen. Take notes. Listen some more. Get clarification. Know what your company can and cannot do. Challenge the status quo. Suggest a solution. Have a conversation.

Find out what's bothering your prospects. Many times they can and will tell you what you need to do to be successful landing their account – you just have to ask. A conversation is the best way I have figured out to make this happen.

Talk with your customers; not at them.

Have a plan for every call.

Success is not about winging it. Success requires dedication and hard work. Do not become a professional greeter. Your customers may enjoy your company but you are wasting their time if you do not come prepared for every call. Ask yourself: "Why am I here? What do I hope to accomplish?" Lead the sales call in that direction. Do this for every call and you will be among the Top Performers.

Sales isn't for everybody.

I could make the argument that we are all in sales, but this is about the true sales professional. You must handle rejection well. You must be curious. Having a servant's heart is helpful. You must enjoy interacting with people and be slow to judge. If you do not possess these traits I would suggest another career path.

Adopt a positive attitude.

Smile. Often.

A pleasant demeanor opens many doors. Why the furrowed brow? You have the best job there is! You control your destiny. You set your income. Rejoice. Smile. Your good attitude is infectious. Your smile is your calling card. Make your prospects curious about why you are so happy. Make them want to talk to you.

Decide today that you will project an air of exuberance to all you meet.

Are you an order taker?

Anyone can fill out an order form. The internet has proven that.

If you are not providing value to your customers you will lose your orders to the lowest priced competitor. Your customers will order many of the same items repeatedly; it is your job to uncover what they are not buying from you; to study their business and offer the solutions you have. None of us have customers that purchase everything from us; yet, that is the goal of every sales professional.

Is your book of business an untapped treasure trove of opportunities? If you sell only the same items week after week, month after month to the same customers - you are an order taker and need to change.

Study your customer's business and be prepared to provide solutions.

Never say never.

In life. In business. In selling.

The timing may be off today but do not discount it for tomorrow. This is an important concept for your success. It may require you to take a pause or a step back to achieve your goal later.

Your prospect may have conflicting priorities. Your project may not be the most important item on their agenda (imagine that).

You may need to rethink your strategy or proposal. Do not set self-imposed limitations. Whatever you put your mind to you can accomplish. Be creative. Be ingenious.

If a prospect doesn't buy from you now that simply means you have more time to understand their needs and provide a solution.

Network within your own company.

Every company has people within its various
departments who get things done. Content
experts. Process experts. Folks who know the
policies and procedures and how to sometimes
work around them. Seek them out. Nurture your
relationships with them. Offer your help. You will
be known as someone who makes things happen.

Change is a fact of life.

Never get too comfortable with the way things are. I guarantee you they will change. Sometimes for the better. Sometimes for the worse. Prepare yourself for the change that is coming. Capitalism is the practice of creative destruction. We build things only to tear them down and reconstruct them with a better idea. Do you track the trends in your industry? Have you prepared yourself to have the skills necessary for the future?

How will you recover from your mistakes?
(You're going to make them)

You will make mistakes. Some pretty spectacular ones. I have. What is your recovery plan? Have you thought about how you might handle a potentially ruinous error? Will you attempt to deflect blame or spin the effect?

Always be honest with those affected by your error. Do not attempt to gloss it over. Be prepared to offer a solution. Follow through on that solution. And learn from it.

Ten little customers are better than one big one.

We all want the big fish. And they should be on your target list. Big fish take time. Losing a big fish is devastating. Work on landing the little ones while you are working on the big one. Little ones are often overlooked nuggets of opportunity your competition walks by every day. They are often less demanding and more profitable.

Know your competitors.

Find out the strengths and weaknesses of your competition: what they do well; what they do poorly; who their good reps are; who their poor reps are. Use this information to differentiate your company, your products and yourself.

Read their catalogs, study their websites and talk to their customers. Often times you'll learn something you can apply to your own situation.

Refrain, however, from criticizing them. Reps who criticize their competitors look weak and unprofessional. Your competitors should make you better.

I've never sold anybody anything. I have had people buy from me.

The phrase, "selling somebody something" carries the connotation that you coerced him or her into a decision they normally would not have made. Someone buying from you denotes it was his or her decision. I believe this is a distinction you should embrace. Position yourself as an expert conveying knowledge that your customers acquire to make a buying decision. Present all the known facts and let them come to a conclusion. Do not force yourself or your solution upon them. Most of us have experienced a "hard sell". This is not the behavior of a sales professional.

If you say you're going to do something, do it.

This is so obvious; yet, I observe sales reps violating it every day.

If you told the customer you would have your price quote to them by Friday – get it to him by Friday. Better yet – Thursday. If you said their samples would arrive by Tuesday – they better arrive by Tuesday.

You are selling yourself as much as you are your product and company. If the customer cannot count on you, why should they believe they can count on your product or service? Your word should be your greatest strength. You are the face of your organization.

Sales is a relationship built upon trust.

Take notes.

Seems obvious, but I have worked with reps who meet with their customers, don't take notes, and claim they never forget anything.

They forget.

You will also. In addition, if you take notes and file them you can refer to them later. Many times I have referenced notes I took months before and found critical information that helped me. Plus it shows interest and respect for your customer's time.

Be resourceful.

The best reps always are. I get very frustrated working with someone who gives up at the first sign of difficulty.

Roadblocks are opportunities to test your mettle. The best opportunities are not always found at the front door. Gatekeepers are put in place for the unimaginative. Sometimes the best opportunities are not the obvious ones. Be resilient.

Consider every set-back an opportunity because many of your competitors will give up.

If your company can't do what your customer needs, recommend one that can. They will buy from you in the future.

Some of my best customers are those I've told not to purchase certain items from me. For whatever reason, I knew they would be disappointed. It took me a while to learn this. Early in my career, I would attempt to sell everything available, even if I did not possess the skill set necessary or my company did not have the expertise. I lost creditability and learned an important lesson: do what is right. In the long term, you will be rewarded. The key is to be a resource for your customer; a trusted advisor; someone who has their interests in mind.

Don't suggest a product just because your company is promoting it or it is new. Suggest the product that is right for your customer.

Don't fall into this trap. I worked for a company that launched two or three new products every month. Our tasks as field sales reps were to sell these products. I often made the mistake of selling them to customers that really did not need them. Your job as a sales professional is to uncover your customer's needs and suggest the correct solution. Not today's special.

Be helpful.

Zig Ziglar has it right. Help enough people and you too will be successful. Don't just be helpful for your customers – be helpful for your co-workers as well. If you know how to do something that they don't – teach them. If you have an internal contact in a certain department – share. Your helpfulness will be rewarded.

Expand your vocabulary. Words mean things. Knowing the right ones can make all the difference.

I subscribe to Merriam-Webster's word of the day. It is in my inbox by 5 AM each morning. There is a dictionary on my desk. Sales requires public speaking; conveying a message. An expanded vocabulary will allow you to communicate more effectively your message and will lead to more sales.

A carefully crafted sentence will convey the exact message you intend. A haphazard string of words will only serve to confuse.

No one cares what you did yesterday.

If you are constantly reliving past victories it might
be because you aren't having any today. In the
business world, no one really cares what you did
yesterday. You may get a pat on the back and a
nice plaque, but you are still expected to perform
now. If you find yourself resting on your laurels,
stop. Make plans on how you are going to succeed
now. Revisit past victories only as a way of
learning how to use them for future ones.

Make mistakes. Learn from them. Make more mistakes.

Experience does not come from the years passing. Experience comes from trying something that did not work and remembering that later.

I often say: "If I haven't made 2 mistakes by noon, I haven't tried very hard."

The timid earn no great rewards. Be bold. Be daring. Try something new.

Sometimes you have to follow.

Sometimes you just have to do what you're told to do.

In business; in life.

You may not agree with the decision; you may have a compelling argument; you might even be right. Doesn't matter. Part of good leadership is following directives.

You also may not have all the information that lead to the decision.

You want to be a great leader: learn to follow

Are you working on your weaknesses?

Do you know what they are? I am a shy person.
Not exactly the trait you'd want for a sales career. I
have forced myself to do presentations in front of
large groups to improve myself. Slowly, over the
years, I have become more comfortable. I still get
butterflies every time before I speak, but I've
learned to control those emotions. What are you
working on?

Are you making excuses or are you making plans?

You just lost your biggest customer. Your sales are down 10%. You aren't hitting your quota.

What are you doing about it?

Ever notice how the mediocre reps have an endless supply of excuses? It's the economy. It's their territory. It's the competition. It's the company's product….Even the worst economic times present opportunities for those willing to look for them. Often times, during a recession many prospects who would not agree to see you will agree to see you now as they are looking at every option. Every territory has untapped areas. Every account has penetration opportunities. Every competitor has a weakness.

What are you planning to do to be successful?

Making excuses is your lack of commitment to excellence.

After every call, I always ask myself: "What did I learn?" If you can't answer that, it was not a productive call.

Questions. Questions. Questions. The key to sales success. You cannot ask too many questions. Rare is the prospect who does not enjoy discussing himself or his company. Learn something on every call. Use it to move the sales process along for your next call. Your success will be in direct correlation to the number of questions you ask. Knowledge of your customers is key to your success.

Sometimes prospects say no just to see if you'll come back.

Many prospects have a revolving door of sale rep after sales rep plying their wares. Why should he buy from you if doesn't know if you are trustworthy and diligent? One way for him to find out is to see if you'll come back. Be the rep that comes back. Time and again. Until you land the sale. Put yourself in your prospects world: rep after rep presenting their products. How do they determine the good reps from the bad? Sometimes their only barometer is persistence.

The best rep doesn't always make the best manager.

The skill set necessary to be an exemplary rep is not the same as what is needed to be an exemplary manager. Yet companies often make this mistake. They promote their best rep to management. Two things happen: They've lost their best rep and their newly promoted manager is often frustrated. What made him a good rep is not helping him to deal with the trials of managing people.

The best rep thinks everyone is a Top Performer and can't understand why they're not. A good manager realizes everyone has value, not all can be A players and that his job is to stretch everyone's individual comfort zone. A Top Performer often doesn't have the temperament to nurture along a B Player.

Don't think you have to aspire to management to be successful. Being a successful sales rep is being successful. Don't let someone else determine what success is.

**Do you associate with the Top Performers?
Or are you with the whiners, the excuse
makers, the complainers?**

I have always sought out the top professionals,
managers, and employees within all of the
organizations I have been associated with. They
are a wealth of information and insight. Little is
more satisfying than to make a joint sales call with
a sales professional and just observe their skills. I
have been nearly in awe and learned to emulate
their approaches. I would not have had many of
my opportunities if not for my associations.

Do you look professional?

What you project to the world is what comes back to you. An aura of professionalism leads to opportunities unavailable to the slouch. To be considered a professional you must act like one. Polite. Courteous. Knowledgeable. Dress appropriately. Observe your competitors and others in related industries for guidance.

Guard your reputation. Respect, once lost, is nearly impossible to regain.

This is true within your company as it is with your customers and prospects. Respect is earned slowly and lost immediately. It is an account that once withdrawn from is hesitant to accept new deposits. Do not succumb to the unethical deal. You will be rightfully passed over for promotion. You will not be considered for the coveted assignments. Your reputation is key to your success.

Do not tolerate disrespectful customers.

You should never tolerate disrespectful or abusive behavior from your customers. Ever. I have had General Managers scream at me. I have had Executive Chefs threaten me. I have had Purchasing Managers call me names. I tolerated this early in my career. You should not. There is never justification for this type of conduct.

Aspire to be an optimist.

The glass will always be half-full. I always see the silver lining. There is always light at the end of the tunnel. If this is not second nature to you, you can train yourself to see the bright side. I am not advocating Pollyannaism but, rather, an outlook that considers the positive first.

A setback is no more than an opportunity to move forward again.

A positive outlook leads to a positive attitude yielding positive results.

It is far easier to complain; to wish it were another way; to blame someone other than you – the truly successful know they have complete control over how they deal with setbacks.

Treat your setbacks as part of your journey towards success.

March to your own drummer.

I am not advocating that you stop shaving and wear bell bottom jeans to work. What I am suggesting is you be yourself. Find your voice. Until I learned my sales presentation should be a conversation I gave a canned speech that was awful. It was painful for me and painful for the customer. Now that I have found my voice and am comfortable in my own skin my sales calls are enjoyable. Be yourself. The true Sales Professional is genuine to himself.

After every sales call, you should have work to do. (And if you're really good, the customer has work to do too.)

I call it homework.

Recap for yourself and your customer what each of you is going to accomplish before your next meeting. This serves as verification of what happened and gives you a reason to return. This is the essence of a productive call. You have moved the process along and are that much closer to the sale. Otherwise, you are nothing more than a professional visitor – checking in – seeing how things are going and never closing the sale.

Choose your battles carefully.

This has taken me the longest to learn. Early in my career, I wanted to right every wrong. I would expend lots of energy and emotion. Mostly, the errors were not corrected. The policy did not change. The company even survived despite my predictions it would not. I do not sign the front of my paycheck. I do not own the company I work for. I am not the CEO. My guess is, neither are you. Be very careful when butting heads with corporate bureaucracy. Some things just are. They don't always make sense, but if in the scheme of things changing them isn't going to make that much difference – leave it alone. You have only so much political capital to expend in a career. Choose to spend it carefully.

The best advice I could give someone new to the corporate world: Learn what your job is; learn what your company expects from you; do what you're told. Leave those battles to someone else.

Anticipate your boss's needs.

If he asks for the same report every Friday – send it to him on Thursday evening. If you have a review coming up – send him a synopsis of your accomplishments. Managers loathe constantly reminding their reps to fill out their paperwork. If, however, he doesn't have to remind you, it will be noticed. You will be considered for the plumb new accounts. Your name will come up during promotion discussions.

Do not use your expense account to supplement your income.

Why would you fudge your expenses? How much extra money could you possibly make? Enough to replace your salary? Trust me you will get caught and you will be fired. I have watched many promising people lose their job over theft (that's really what it is). Padding your expenses is stealing. Don't do it.

If you can justify being dishonest with your expense report – what else are you willing to be dishonest about?

Live your life without regret.

Do the things you want to do. Do not wait for tomorrow or next week or next year. Plan to do them now. I have few regrets; that may be why, at my core, I am a happy, satisfied person. Sure, there are plenty of things I'd still like to accomplish, but I have a plan to do all of them. Don't look back on your life and wish you'd done things differently. Start today and take control. Do not lament what you haven't done. Go do it.

Everyone is replaceable.

None of us are as good as we think we are. None of us are *the* reason our customers buy from us. (I've only worked with one rep in 25 years who actually took a majority of his customers with him.)

The moment you think you're not replaceable is the moment you lose touch with reality and potentially could be replaced. Realize the CEO, the Vice President of Sales, your Sales Manager, and *you*, are all replaceable tomorrow. The key to success is to provide value so your company does not want to replace you. Make yourself an integral part of your company's business plan. Make your name come up when new initiatives are considered. Always be thinking how you can assist with your company's success.

And if you are let go, you have marketable skills other employers desire. Never get too comfortable. Comfort can breed complacency which can lead to laziness and bad habits. You need a fire in your belly every morning to be a successful sales professional.

Look for the good in others.

Every person has good qualities. Every person has a gift. Every person has something unique to them. Find that. Always assume everyone you come across is inherently good. Your rewards will be ample. You will learn things the gloomy people never will.

Respect your competitors.

To me, nothing is quite as unprofessional as disparaging your competition. Do not denigrate the people or the companies you compete against. You only make yourself look bad. Your competitors are in business just like you are; if they weren't any good at what they did they wouldn't still be in business. It is lazy to put your competitors down. It demonstrates a weak salesperson. Top Performers recognize the good qualities of their competitors and never put them down.

Learn from your competitors. There are things they do better than you. Copy their successes. Highlight what your company does better or different.

Don't accept mediocrity.

I strive to do the best I can in every situation. You should also. Why waste your time? I also strive to improve myself. Do not strive to be adequate. Strive to be great. This is a mindset that requires excellence for all you do. You need to have the commitment to work hard and endeavor to be the best.

The acceptance of mediocrity will be your downfall.

If you are not passionate about what you do, do something else.

I can't wait to get up in the morning and start a new day. If you find yourself dreading to come to work it is time to consider a career change. You should enjoy what you do. It should come easily to you. It should not be "work". It should inspire you to want to do the best you can. Passion breeds success. I have had jobs where I had to convince myself to go to work each day. If this is you, commit yourself now to finding a career you are thrilled to be a part of.

You should want to come to work. One of my sayings is: "Everyday is Friday at _____." Is every day Friday for you? Or is it Monday?

Sales people need an upbeat environment in order to thrive.

Is there a buzz in your office? Can you feel the excitement? Is there palpable anticipation for the next big win? If not, you had better do something about that and quickly. Nothing kills a sales organization faster than negativity. Morale is a fragile object that requires careful cultivation. Don't allow yours to wither from neglect.

As a manager or a rep you are responsible for contributing to the positive environment at your place of work. Be a positive influence.

Make decisions.

You cannot ever make a completely informed decision. Don't try. Make good decisions, not perfect ones. Hesitation is an indication of weakness. Don't always wait for approval. Leaders are decisive. Successful sales reps commit themselves to a course of action and follow through. Decisiveness is a characteristic of a top performer.

Exercise your authority. Stretch it a little on occasion.

Wander around.

Do not park yourself in your office and expect the world to come to you. Get up, and mingle with your people in *their* space. They will be more comfortable and more apt to talk openly with you. You need their feedback. You can learn a lot about your organization by simply observing it. You cannot do that from behind your desk. Good management requires good information. Go learn something about your people and your business. Go on calls with your people.

If you're a rep wander around your accounts. I guarantee you will uncover an opportunity you didn't have a clue about.

Be careful with profanity.

I love to string together a series of expletives. They
can roll off my tongue like a salt-crusted sailor.
The business world is not the place for such
language. You portray yourself as vulgar and
unimaginative. Act the professional you are in all
settings. If you must use profanity do so carefully
and infrequently.

Be the professional you are.

Complain up.

If you are a manager, do not voice your grievances to your people. Your role is to be a buffer, a wall that filters out the unnecessary noise; not a megaphone that amplifies it. Nothing is more unprofessional than a leader who disrupts morale by complaining about company issues. If you have concerns, air them with your boss, privately. Your people look to you for guidance and leadership.

If you are a rep, don't complain to your peers. Standing around criticizing your company accomplishes nothing. Make a business case for each item you wish to discuss; vocalize it and move on. Trust your boss and your company to work to fix those problems. (Know everything cannot be resolved.)

Defend your people.

If you are a manager one of your most important roles is to be the voice for your people. Your success is wholly dependent upon them. You are their guardian. Shield them from the unnecessary noise of corporate bureaucracy and policy. They do not need to know all that goes on behind the scenes. Act as a filter so that the positive is accentuated.

Do not pass on rumor or gossip. Focus on the goals at hand.

Utilize your commute to better yourself.

The average commute is around 30 minutes each way. That is a gift of an hour each day to learn something. You could dramatically increase your expertise in your field in a year just utilizing your commute time; learn a language; listen to motivational tapes.

Do not mindlessly listen to music.

There are a host of companies that provide access to content for you to listen to while on your way to work: business book summaries; motivational speakers (John Maxwell, Earl Nightingale, Zig Ziglar are a couple of my favorites). Subscriptions are very affordable. Money well spent.

Give up that expensive cup of coffee and listen to the leaders in your field.

If you are a leader, lead.

You were given your position of authority, so exercise it. Decide what it is you want to accomplish and lead the charge. Take the hill. Do not wait for permission. Companies want their managers to take control. Decide today what is important and lead your team towards that goal.

If you are a rep, take charge. Your book of business is yours to manage. Commit yourself to be responsible for your accounts. Your company has given you an opportunity to sell a product or service, marketing materials to assist you and a group of customers to call on. All at no cost to you. It is like being a franchisee without any outlay of capital. Do something with that opportunity.

Price will always be an issue.

Customers buy three things from you: price, service, and results.

Your job, as a sales professional, is to shift the focus from price to service and results.

There will *always* be competitors who will offer a lower price.

Differentiate yourself from your competition to provide value to justify a higher price. Value is comprised of the services you provide and the results your products offer your customer. Don't confuse price with value. A lower priced item or service can, and often does, cost more. A lower priced item often is bereft of additional services.

If your service is industry leading, focus on that. (Consider Fed Ex versus UPS). If your products produce results different from your competitors, focus on that (Consider Apple versus Microsoft).

Anyone can sell on price. Sales professionals sell value. Value has no set price.

Never take credit for something you didn't do.

Why would you? Particularly if you are in a management position. Your people's success is your success. This is the quickest morale breaker there is. If your people can't trust you why would they follow you? Too many managers think their people's success is detrimental to their own. Nothing could be further from reality. I always tried to surround myself with people smarter than me and I never took credit for their good works. Don't fall into this trap.

Praise in public. Reprimand in private.

You should praise often. And specifically. Telling
someone they did a good job is nice; telling them
how they did a good job builds confidence and
assures you they will strive to keep being
exemplary. Reprimanding someone in public, even
in a closed-door meeting, is unprofessional and
breeds morale issues.

Give back.

Share the rewards of your success. Whether you donate your time and money to a charity or mentor a new employee you need to give of yourself. Do not be selfish with the fruits of your success. Sharing your success leads to others success. I do believe a good sales rep needs to be a little selfish; however, all top performers give of themselves. Strive to devote yourself to giving back.

Sharing your good fortune exponentially adds to your success. Always.

There are three sides to every story.

Your rep's story.

The customer's story.

And, what actually happened.

People have a natural tendency to embellish a situation in their favor. Do not allow your prejudices to let you jump to conclusions. Gather all the information you can and apply your judgment. Do not automatically assume your rep or your customer is right. More than likely the truth is somewhere in the middle.

Consider this when dealing with a customer's complaint. They will explain it to their benefit.

Sometimes, all you have to do is listen.

People get frustrated. Often they simply need to verbalize their concerns. Whether it is your reps or your customers venting, be careful not to try and always solve the situation. They may not want a solution. They may just need to communicate their frustrations. Actively listening may be all you need to do. Don't be too quick with an answer. Listen. Be empathetic. Let them vent.

What motivates you?

You need to know this, as it is not someone else's job to motivate you. You need to motivate yourself. Sure, your manager may work to motivate you; but to be truly successful, you need to strive to succeed on your own. Spend some time considering what it is that motivates you. Is it money? Is it reaching your goals? Is it providing for your family? Is it winning the respect of your peers? Is it solving your customer's problems? All are worthy accomplishments. Plan your day, your week, your month and your year around performing the activities that will cause you to strive to do your best.

Don't let fear motivate you. Joy should be the outcome of what you do.

You will have setbacks.

You may be passed over for a promotion you believe you deserve.
Someone else may be assigned the coveted account you know should be yours.
Your company may go through a reorganization.
You may lose an account to a competitor where you had the better offer.
You might get demoted.

Setbacks are to be expected.
How will you handle them?
What is your plan?
What will be your attitude?
Have you prepared yourself for the unexpected?

Sometimes you have to take a step back to take two steps forward. Sometimes the obvious path is blocked and you will have to go around. Do not be surprised by the disappointments that are going to occur in your career. Equip yourself to handle them. Focus on the positive. Learn from the experience.

Be responsive.

Customers want you to get back to them within a
reasonable time. Even if it's just letting them know
you are working on their concern and don't have an
answer yet.
They need to know they can count on you. Don't
make them wait; it only provides an opportunity for
your competitors.

Under commit. Over deliver.

This is not meant to be deceptive. Rather, it is a mindset where your goal is to exceed your customer's expectations. A willingness to do whatever it takes. I have loaded my car with product on many occasions and made deliveries. You need to cultivate your servant's heart. A successful sales rep serves his customers. It needs to be done with grace with no sense of obligation to your client. It should be a natural extension of your character. Your customers should be delighted with your service.

I continue to be amazed by the number of sales reps who do not adhere to this adage. They want the sale so they commit to something they know will take a herculean effort to accomplish. "I will find out" or "I am not sure we can…." are perfectly acceptable answers to customer demands.

Don't worry.

To me, worry is a futile emotion. There can be no positive outcome associated with worrying. If you spend an inordinate amount of time worrying it is probably because your life has no plan and you are allowing things to happen to you.

Take charge; control your future; make plans and commit to carrying them out.

Worry is for the undisciplined. Planning and discipline eradicate worry.

Be early.

This is a discipline of the true professional. You are in sales; you cannot be late. Your tardiness reflects your lack of commitment to your prospect's business.

There is no excuse. Plan for the unexpected. Visit a new client's location the day before the appointment to make sure you know how to get there and where to park. Give yourself extra time between appointments.

This is more than a common courtesy; this is a discipline. It conveys to your prospect that you value their time and their business.

Question your assumptions.

I believe I can read people. I am right about 40% of the time, but I think I'm right 90% of the time. I have learned to make myself examine my preconceptions.

Do not make the mistake of assuming your way out of a sale. Question everything you *think* you know. Know what you know. Find out what you don't.

.

Accept responsibility.

Do not make excuses. A professional stands up and accepts what is his. If you find yourself blaming the economy or your territory or your company for your lack of success – stop. Examine the actual cause of your failure – you. Commit to improving your skills, your actions and your attitude. You control the facets of your success. You determine the behaviors you will exhibit. Do not allow yourself to make excuses; scrutinize your performance with a critical eye, always looking for improvement.

Ask for the order.

I have watched too many sales reps give excellent presentations only to forget this most critical step. Sometimes you have to be blunt. Don't prolong your sales process by not asking your customer for the order. Commit yourself to this behavior; make it a natural part of your presentation. If you don't get the order, ask what it would take to get their business. This can provide invaluable information as it requires the customer to consider why they are buying from your competitor. Many times this is the last, critical step necessary for you to land the business.

Continue to ask for the order. Never assume that because a customer purchased from you today that they will tomorrow.

Companies have a code of ethics, you should too.

You need to have a set of principles that are ironclad; a moral compass to guide you on your journey. Do not allow yourself to get caught up in the moment and drift from your values. Listen to the voice inside you when he whispers words of warning. A Sales Professional does not tolerate dishonest business of any kind.

Sales is an emotional process.

As much as you would like to believe your customers and prospects base their decisions on logical, sound business reasons – they often don't. Many times they will stay with their incumbent vendor simply based upon familiarity. Or not change based upon a fear of looking bad. Or they are not convinced your offer/company/proposal is that much different than their current vendor. Your job is to belay these fears and make your customers look good. They must know their decision to utilize you will enhance their position. That your offer *will* save them money. Your offer *will* improve efficiencies. As salespeople, we tend to inflate our company's differentiators. Most customers see few differences in the offerings of two competing companies. Make sure the differences you *do* highlight are significant.

Your customers have egos and anxiety. Do not lose sight of the emotional component of the sales process. However, do not let emotion color *your* process. Frustrations and setbacks are simply an integral part of the profession.

Don't set self-imposed limitations.

You need to stretch to be successful. Don't assume you can't land a coveted account because of some outside factor. If your offering is attractive enough, they will figure out a way to buy from you. The world will present you with plenty of limitations – do not add to them. Be open to new ideas, new ways of doing things. The true sales professional is always looking to upgrade himself.

I used to always carry a Day-Timer and was never interested in electronic time management. I had to write it down. Now everything I plan is in Outlook. It is far more efficient than a Day-Timer and I can now share my schedule with others at my company. I adapted to the new normal. You need to as well. What are you doing today that is limiting your success? Change it now.

Details are not glamorous

Making phone calls.
Unanswered voicemails.
The follow-up emails.
Studying your customer's business.
Gaining approval for the deal
The presentations.
Waiting for a decision.

None of it is exciting; mostly it is mundane. It is, however, necessary.

There are no overnight successes.

There is no achievement without effort.

The best make it look effortless because of the countless hours spent honing their skill.

Handling the details is a requirement for your success.

Your customers are your competitors' prospects.

What are you doing to give your competitors an opening? Taking your customers for granted? Not communicating with them? Assuming all is well? Being an order taker? Not providing value? Not providing information on new products and services? Don't ever think that your competitors aren't calling on your customers. Sometimes your customers will tell you, sometimes they won't. Always assume they won't.

Never take a current customer for granted. Never think they won't entertain an offer from one of your competitors. Treat them as if they were still a prospect – and you stand a good chance they won't become one.

Trust your gut

Each of us has a small voice inside of us that gains
its expression from our experiences. Those
experiences provide us with knowledge that leads
to wisdom and sound decision making. Be quiet
and still enough each day so that you can hear that
small voice inside of you.

Trust what it is telling you.

Good things happen when you see your customers.

We live in an ever-expanding digital age. Facebook, Twitter, E-Mail, Text-Messaging, CRM Software.....all grab our time and keep us from interacting, *in person*, with our customers. There is no substitute for a face-to-face meeting to deepen your relationship. E-Mails are so easily misunderstood. (I have an unwritten rule that after three back and forth emails - I pick up the phone and call the person.) We're all so harried – rushing from one task to the next - constantly in touch with each other (digitally) yet so isolated. Go see your customers. In their space. Wander around – learn something about their business that no amount of googling would ever tell you.

Listen. Recognize that you aren't very good at it.

Sales people are gregarious, outgoing, *people* people. We tell stories. We laugh. We carry on. Discipline yourself to let your customers and prospects talk more than you do. You can't listen with your mouth open.

Remember to listen to gain understanding and insight. Not so that you can reply.

Do you sign the front of your paycheck?

Almost all of us sign the back of our paychecks. If you're in that majority you are obligated to follow company policy; complete your reports; meet your quota, and generally do what you're told to do. Being a good soldier is an integral part of being successful within any organization. (We can't all be president.)

The higher you rise in an organization, surprisingly, the greater the expectation that you will follow company policy. Vice Presidents establish policy; middle managers enforce it and you, the sales professional, are expected to follow it. (Don't think your quota achievement excuses you from the rules.)

Don't like it? Start your own company. (I'll bet you'll have rules.)

As a manager, your job is to get the work done.

Resist the temptation to do the work. You know you can do it better; faster and with fewer errors. That's not your job anymore. Your job is to see the work gets done. On time. With as few mistakes as possible.

Teach your people to do the work to your level of expertise and then you'll have a whole team of experts.

Your success is determined by your team's success. Your team's success is determined by the training, coaching, and support you give them. Not by doing the work yourself.

Why do we believe everything our prospects tell us?

"Your price is too high." "Give me a price list and I will get back to you." "I have your proposal and I need a couple weeks to digest it."

Don't you think they tell every salesperson that their price is too high? Or if you give them a price list they will just take it to their incumbent supplier and ask for price relief on the items your company is lower on? Do you really think they are carefully considering your proposal?

It is hard to change vendors. For *anything*. You have to give your prospect a compelling reason, a *really* compelling reason to change. You need to assess your prospect's condition like a doctor assesses their patients: ask questions; make no assumptions; probe deeper into the responses received; reject false information.

Challenge your prospects to truly consider your offering. Challenge yourself to truly know your prospects' business.

Don't get overwhelmed

You have a very detailed RFP with a short
response time.
You have a large project with required inputs from
many departments.
Your boss wants a detailed report on your mid-year
results.

All due in the same week.

You will have to break this up and work on parts of
each project. Don't get overcome by the *amount* of
work; just get to work.

Best Question Never Asked.

"Is there anything else you wish to get out of this meeting?"

We think we have the prospect all figured out. We've brainstormed; strategized; built an agenda; and a beautiful deck with an outstanding solution.

You may have missed a key component.

Always ask – is there anything else?

You are not as busy as you think you are.

Sales reps are an odd lot. I've never met a sales rep who isn't overworked, underpaid and too busy for anything new.

Ask yourself: is that really true?

An opportunity with a huge upside and a tight deadline presents itself - funny how you find time to complete it. Friday afternoon comes – you sign off early to......play golf.....visit friends.......shop....

We find time for what is important to us. The key to success is using your time to do what's important. What time-wasters are affecting you? How often do you check social media? How much television do you watch?

What could you do today to give yourself an extra 30 minutes?

Now that you have those 30 minutes – what are you going to do with it?

Objections are buying signals.

You're sailing through your sales presentation. Heads are nodding. You're feeling good. Then you get hit with an objection.

Don't let that derail your presentation. Plan for objections. Prepare your answers. Remember an objection from a customer is not an indication of uninterest; it is a request for clarification – they want more information so they can better understand and consider your proposal.

An interested customer wants to know more; an uninterested customer does not.

Do the circumstances of today dictate your actions?

The stock market tumbles. Do you panic and sell your carefully diversified portfolio? Your company's sales soften. Do you hastily reorganize in an untested effort to realize sales growth? You are not closing accounts and are getting pressure from your sales manager to hit your number. Do you begin to pressure your prospects?

I see it happen over and over. A company; a division; a sales team or a sales person is not meeting revenue targets. The message goes out: "Get the sale. Do whatever you need to do. We're not hitting our targets. We need sales."

So companies, divisions, sales teams and sales reps begin to veer from time-proven practices. They don't spend the time to understand their customers' needs. They don't craft a solution. They push. They take shortcuts. Many land the sale. The month or the quarter might be saved. But at what cost? You pressed a customer to buy from you; maybe you cut your price; maybe you exaggerated the features of your product. Is this truly a prudent way to conduct long-term sustainable business?

Do not allow yourself to get caught in this trap. Time tested, proven sales methodologies of getting to understand your customer's business and their challenges to craft a solution always work. Don't allow yourself to deviate from what you know you should do as a salesperson.

You've lost your best customer. Now what?

How you handle this, in large part, will determine your long term success.

You could allow emotions to influence your reaction and disparage the customer for making a horrendous choice, or you could bad mouth the new vendor. You could make the transition difficult or raise your prices or demand different payment terms. All of which you could justify in your mind to punish the customer for choosing someone other than you.

Or.

You could immediately meet with the customer. Thank him for his business. Assure him you will make the transition seamless and easy. And commit to him that if things do not work out you will gladly reinstate him as a customer.

Which option do you think will better position you for long-term success?
Which option positions you as the sales professional you aspire to be?

E-mail.

Does it manage you? Or do you manage it?

When did we decide emails warranted an
instantaneous response?
Do your customers and co-workers expect an
immediate reply? Why?

E-mail is an amazing tool. It can increase your
productivity exponentially. Misused, however, it
can suck us into a vortex of a never-ending grind.
Additionally, instant responses do not allow for
careful reflection.

Set aside time each day to work through your
inbox. If presented with a complex situation or a
pressing issue allow yourself time for consideration
of different options.

Don't allow yourself to get caught in the trap of an
endless series of replies. Pick up the phone and
call the person. Often a 30-second conversation
solves an issue that 17 emails cannot.

Give yourself permission for the 24-hour rule: I
have 24 hours to respond to an email I receive. If
the issue is more pressing than that your co-
workers and customers should be calling you. If
you are answering every email within 15 minutes of
receiving it you are allowing your inbox to manage
you.

Try this for a week. At first, it will be very tempting to continue with your old habits. I guarantee you if you are disciplined and follow this guidance your productivity will improve and your stress level will be reduced.

Good luck.

Discipline separates the average from the outstanding.

What really makes someone successful? Talent plays a role. Luck and circumstance can play a role.

But what really defines the successful from the ordinary is discipline.

Discipline to make cold calls.
Discipline to follow up.
Discipline to spend the time and effort to practice.
Discipline to continue to learn.
Discipline to do what you say you are going to do.

Your innate talents will only take you so far. The blessings of good timing eventually run their course. Do you want to count yourself among the top achievers? Have the discipline to do what needs to be done. Each and every day.

Fail your way to success

The safe way is the path to mediocrity. To be successful you have to take chances. You have to take risks. Sometimes you will fail.

Michael Jordan was cut from his high school basketball team.
J.K. Rowling was rejected by 12 publishers.
Dr. Seuss's first book was rejected by 27 publishers.
Oprah Winfrey was demoted from her job as a TV anchor.

Imagine if they hadn't continued to pursue their dreams.

Don't be afraid to fail. Failure is part of your path to success.

Control your emotions.

We are emotional beings. We experience fear, anger, excitement, joy, disappointment….in our personal as well as our professional lives. What separates the outstanding from the average is our reaction to those emotions.

You don't get the promotion you believe you've earned. Do you allow your disappointment to cloud your judgment and react with hurt and anger? Or do you realize that decisions made above you often involve information you are not aware of? There could be other considerations that led to the decision not to promote you at this time.

Someone else is given the prime new account. You feel strongly it should be yours based on your performance. Is your reaction to march into your manager's office and demand the account be given to you? A better plan might be to professionally ask what parameters led to the decision. Maybe there is another project they have in mind for you? Reacting with anger over the loss of the recently acquired account will most likely eliminate the possibility of working on any coveted new projects.

I am not suggesting that you stifle your passion. Or your enthusiasm. To be truly an outstanding competitor you need drive, desire, and commitment. Those emotions support you well during your successes; they can be a hindrance during your setbacks.

Work life balance.

The lines of work and personal lives have blurred. Anyone who owns a smartphone has checked a work email on the weekend or after hours. Before the advent of smartphones and e-mails, it was not possible to work weekends and nights without physically being at the office.

So we work all the time and work where we are.

Companies have certainly enjoyed the increase in productivity this brings, often without paying for it. It is expected that if you have company e-mail and a smartphone that you are available all the time. You aren't paid for this availability, but it is an expectation most employers have.

No one seems to be discussing the benefits to the employee this arrangement brings. You can run errands during the day because you are not expected to be at the office. You can schedule doctor's appointments when it is convenient. You can work at the coffee shop; the library; the beach; your home; the pool.....
You can pick your kids up after school. You can coach your kids' soccer team.

Why is it only your employer's responsibility to maintain a proper work/life balance? You need to work to establish your own boundaries.

Time for reflection.

Do you give yourself time for reflection? Do you set aside time each day; each week to reflect on your goals?

If you are simply rushing from one task to another through the course of your days, when do you have time to consider the big picture? When do you have time to focus on what is important?

Emails; social media; conference calls; meetings – all demand our attention.

To truly know if the path you're on is the right path you need time to consider what you're doing. What is occupying your day? What *should* be occupying your day? Are you so caught up in the details you've lost sight of your goals?

Allow yourself time for quiet reflection. You'll be amazed at the focus you will gain.

Next steps.

You've just met with your customer. The meeting went great. The customer was very engaged – lots of discussion points.

Did you clearly identify next steps?

Does everyone know what they are?

Without clearly defining next steps – and who is responsible – your great customer meeting will have been wasted. Don't be afraid to communicate next steps verbally *and* in written form.

Do you interrupt?

To be successful in sales you have to listen.

If you are interrupting your customers to make your next point or offer your solution – stop. Listen. Reflect. Consider.

Don't be so quick to talk. Give your customer a chance to detail their issue.

The best solutions to your customer's problems come from a clear understanding of their situation, which can only occur if you listen closely to them.

Consolidation. Good or bad?

Four airlines now control 80% of all domestic flights.

16 Companies now control most of what you buy
("These 16 companies control almost everything you buy":
Marina Nazaro *Business Insider* Oct 17, 2015)

Consolidation allows companies to reduce costs and be more efficient.

But it reduces choices.

And it creates bureaucracy. And inflexible policies.

Does it also create opportunities?

Opportunities to fill an unmet need?

Opportunities to provide services, customer support and return policies the big competitors do not?

Every business climate offers opportunities.

First Impressions.

Have you stopped to consider how you make a first impression?
We've all heard the adage – "You never get a second chance to make a first impression." – But how do you create a good first impression?

Firm handshake. Look the person in the eye. And most importantly – show genuine interest. It is about them – not you. Resist the urge to talk about yourself – instead, focus on the person you've just met. Don't impatiently wait for them to finish a story just so you can share a similar experience.

First impressions are lasting impressions. Work to make yours positive.

Performance Reviews

Judge how you did; not how you are going to do. Certainly, they can assist in predicting future performance, but they are no guarantee.

As an employee, your performance review is an acknowledgment of the work you have done and how well you've done it. Ideally, they also provide a roadmap for the work to be done in the future and how to excel at that work.

As a manager be sure and recognize the work done for the entire year – not just the last three months. Be fair. Be candid. Be prepared to offer how the employee can improve. Provide direction for the future.

Do not think an exemplary review assures your promotion. Many factors determine who gets promoted.

Periodically self-evaluate yourself. If you were to give yourself your performance review – how would you do? Be brutally honest. You know where you need to improve; you know where you are potentially slacking; you also know what you're good at. Make a plan to improve. Work the plan. Your next evaluation will positively reflect the work you've done.

Sometimes you have to walk away.

What if you don't have what the customer wants?

As a salesperson, your first reaction is to offer them what you have and try and convince the customer that is what they really want.

But isn't that why sales people have a bad reputation?

Sometimes you have to walk away.

Who is your customer's customer?

Stop and think. Who are your customer's customers? What market does your customer serve? What types of customers do they have? What types do they want? What markets are they trying to penetrate?

Why is this important?

What better way is there to tailor your product or service? If you know the types of customers your customer serves you can have a better idea of how your offering will solve their challenges.

What's holding you back?

If we're honest with ourselves, most of us know what needs to be done. We need to make that phone call; have that difficult conversation; present our ideas; tell a customer no.....but we don't.

Why?

Fear of rejection? Fear of failure? Fear of the unknown? Fear of success?

Not taking action *is* taking action.

Challenge yourself to do one thing each day you've been putting off.

Do you block out time for yourself?

Have you ever opened up your Outlook calendar and thought ugh – how in the world am I going to get everything done? Conference calls. Meetings. Deadlines. Reports……

If you don't discipline yourself to block out time to do the important things – your day will be taken up by others. Take time for yourself. Block out time each day to work on long term projects; to tackle your to-do list. To return phone calls. To reflect.

We all can't be president.

Most of the professional advice I see being peddled today centers around leadership. While it is good advice to work on the skills you will need to be a better leader, remember there are only a small number of leadership positions within any company. You can certainly aspire to climb the company ladder, but know you may not make it up many rungs. Don't be discouraged. Leadership skills are needed at all levels.

Part of being a good leader is being a good follower: to give direction you need to be able to take direction.

Titles convey responsibility. They do not anoint the person with the abilities needed to succeed.

Learn to lead yourself and you may be given the opportunity to lead others.

**If you aren't taking risks, you are leading a
life of mediocrity.**

The easy road yields few rewards. You will never
garner all the information needed to make a risk-
free decision. You can, however, utilize your
experience and the knowledge at hand to make an
informed decision. Business will always be a series
of calculated risks. Do not be afraid to fail. Failure
is key to your success. Failure is the foundation
upon which you build the structure of your
achievements. You cannot succeed without failure.
They are symbiotic. The true Sales Professional
takes risks.

Risks lead to success. Sometimes you stumble
along the way – but you cannot succeed without
risk.

New Year's Resolutions are a waste of time

8% of us actually achieve our resolution. **8%.**

Why pursue something with a 92% failure rate?

If you truly want to change something you need a plan and the discipline to execute that plan.

"I want to lose 25 pounds" is destined for failure.

"I will lose 25 pounds by: working out – eating healthy - taking the stairs." Specific, actionable items that you can measure your progress towards, stand a much better chance of success.

Make this your best year yet.

Why I don't play the lottery.

1:1100 chance a high school senior football player will make it to the NFL.

1:700,000 chance of being struck by lightning in any given year.

1:649,739 chance of drawing a royal flush.

1:292,201,338 chance of winning the Powerball Jackpot.

Invest in yourself; your odds of success are 100%.

Conference calls.

Conference calls have become ubiquitous. Yet the lack of professionalism that I experience on a daily basis amazes me.

Put your phone on mute. Oh my. So rudimentary. Yet almost every conference call with more than 25 people includes someone who did not put their phone on mute. Please mute your phone.

Don't place the conference call on hold. Again almost every conference call with a large audience includes someone who puts the conference call on hold. Now we all get to listen to the hold music. Joy.

Consider your message. Conference calls are great for sharing general information to a large group. They are not appropriate for complicated issues; human resource matters; question and answer for a large group.

If you're the host – have an agenda. Get to the point.

If you're a participant – pay attention. It is rude and unprofessional to attempt to multi-task during a conference call.

Send out post call notes. If you don't have any – why did you have the call?

Plan your day or someone else will

E-mails. Conference calls. Meetings.

Who is planning your day?

Are you simply reacting to what happens?

Or are you planning your day?

Your success is determined by you.

What are you doing today to guide yourself towards your goals?

Take control of your success – don't let the plans of another become yours.

Breaking 80 on the golf course

I just shot a 79. Quite an accomplishment. It made me think about how my work towards breaking 80 applies to the business world.

For years I struggled to break 100. I did not play often; and when I did play I was very inconsistent and very frustrated. A couple years ago I made a conscious decision to get better at golf. That was the goal.

I put a simple plan together working on the aspects of my game. First I needed to drive the ball better. I purchased an offset driver that helped me not slice the ball. I spent a lot of time on the internet looking at different types of swings and how to hit the ball longer and straighter. I made adjustments based upon how I hit the ball and now I can pretty consistently hit a 220-230 yard drive. Not that long – but long enough for the course I play.

Next, I worked on my long irons. I don't hit them well. I took them out of my bag and purchased some hybrids. Made all the difference. I now hit those clubs very well.

Then I worked on my short irons, chipping and putting until I could consistently hit those shots well 80% of the time.

But the biggest change I made was playing the game I have, rather than the game I wish I had. I don't hit the ball very far – in the past I would grab the club, that on my best day, would go the distance I had to hit it. Not surprisingly, I ended up short most of the time. The biggest improvement came when I would go up a club or not try and hit a shot I only could hit one time out of ten. I played the game I have and my scores improved dramatically.

So how does this apply to the business world? First, have a plan – what do you want to accomplish? What is your goal? Making Quota? Being in the top 10% of reps at your company? Decide what your goal is. Then make a plan on how you are going to accomplish that goal. Break it down into the components you need to master to achieve that goal. For golf, for me – it was driving the ball well; realizing I could not hit my long irons and playing the game I have rather than the one I wish I had. Then I had to practice and learn. To achieve sales quota what do you need to do? How many customer appointments do you need to close a sale? You should know this. If it takes 10 appointments to close a sale and you need 2 closes a month – you better have a least 20 appointments each month. What have you learned from the customers who didn't buy from you? What have you learned from the ones that have? Do you practice your craft? Do you make changes to your presentations based on the feedback you get?

I had fun getting better at golf. I had a goal, a plan and practiced. It was fun to see my scores improve. Do the same for your work. And don't forget to have fun

Taking notes.

All good salespeople take notes. Few of us can remember everything. If you think you can – you're wrong – take notes.

I have a suggestion I've learned over the years. Use one notebook for everything. I see lots of people with multiple notebooks – maybe a daytimer for their calendar – then a series of notebooks – maybe even post it notes for a quick thought. Stop. Try using one notebook for everything. For one thing – you will always have the right notebook – with all your notes in it. You won't be scrambling trying to remember if it is in your calendar or your blue notebook or the black one. Saves time. Makes you more organized.

Additionally – take a look at using a Bullet Journal (bulletjournal.com) – I have been using this system for the past three months and I have found it very helpful. You can use your own notebook or purchase one they have available on their website.

If you fall....

Get up, brush yourself off and try again.

My father-in-law owns a cattle ranch outside of Phoenix, AZ. Over the years I have helped him with round up on many occasions. A couple years ago I was there with my youngest daughter Gracie (who was around 13 at the time). We got up early – caught our horses – bridled and saddled them to prepare for the day's ride. I was paired with one of their new horses – Miss July. I bridled and saddled her and mounted up. She started bucking like we were at a rodeo.

Going through my mind at the time was an event that had occurred 20 years previous: me on a bucking horse. After several bucks and the horse not stopping and heading for a grove of mesquite trees I had decided to bail. So I bailed off the back of the horse. Long story short – I ended up breaking both of my wrists.

So fast forward 20 years – horse bucking – not stopping – but we were in a pasture with no trees around. This time, I thought, I am bailing off the front of the horse. So I did. Landed on my face. Wrung my bell a bit. I am laying on the ground checking to see if I am okay and my sister-in-law comes running over and starts praying over me. So now I'm thinking I'm not ok – my face is bashed in or why would she be praying over me. I get up. I'm okay. My family at this point is concerned – wants me to ride a different horse. Nope, I say, I'm getting back on this one. Which I did. Rode all day. Did fine.

Great teaching lesson for my daughter. You get knocked down. You get up. You try again.

There's always more to the story

Someone gets promoted. Someone gets demoted.
Someone gets fired. Your company goes through a
major reorganization. Your company makes a
major policy change. Your company sells a
division. Your company buys a competitor.

You scratch your head because it doesn't seem to
make sense to you. It doesn't seem to add up. The
person fired/demoted seemed to be doing a great
job. The competitor you just purchased isn't doing
well. The old policy worked just fine.

Remember, you only know what you know. There
is always more to the story....often it cannot be
communicated. Or a longer term strategy is at play
and this move is just one of many more to come.
Trust your leadership to be making the right
decisions. Do your best to adapt to the new
situation. Understand the changes and move on.
Do not allow yourself to get mired in the past.
Good companies make changes as they adjust to
the competitive landscape. Good employees
understand this, adapt and continue to provide
value to their organization.

Are you on your phone....

Or are you living life in the present moment?

I travel extensively for my job and I have noticed lately everyone seems to be on their phone all the time. Waiting in the TSA line. Waiting at the gate. Waiting to board the plane. On the plane. Immediately once the plane lands. While eating at a restaurant. In meetings.

How much is life passing you by? How many opportunities to connect or network with others are you missing because you are checking your Facebook page or Twitter feed? When are you taking the time to reflect?

I challenge all of us (and, yes, I am as guilty of this as anyone) to spend 15 minutes a day – disconnected from your phone – and just observe; reflect; connect.

People are selfish

Don't lose sight of this when calling on your customers and prospects. For the most part, they will act in a way that is beneficial to them. Try and think how your product or service will offer a solution that will make them look good.

Flying is magic

A 737 maximum takeoff weight is nearly 80 tons. That is the equivalent of 44 Honda Accords. That is simply amazing. Yet, we take it for granted. We sit bored in our seats, ignoring the safety presentation given by the cabin crew and watch movies as we fly across the sky in a metal tube that really should have never left the ground.

Allow yourself to experience again the child-like wonder associated with everyday things we take for granted: flying, cell phones, electricity, television, and the internet. It will be good for your soul; improve your attitude; and may help you to open your mind to other possibilities.

Reward yourself

For the past ten years, I have wanted to purchase a Karmann Ghia. (I owned one in my twenties and really didn't appreciate it.) This week I finally bought one.

I believe it is important to reward yourself for your accomplishments. Spend some of your money on yourself - whether it is on an impractical car or a pleasure boat or a getaway cabin in the woods - I believe it is vital to your continued success to pause and reward yourself.

What could you spend your hard earned money on that you've been putting off?

Criticism

Most of us, if asked, would say we are performing well. We are doing all that is asked of us in an exemplary fashion. What will you do when faced with feedback that is contrary to your rosy view of yourself? Will you argue? Will you attempt to gloss over your shortcomings? Or will you listen and attempt to make improvements?

Criticism is not meant to tear you down; let it build you up.

Thank You

Thank you so very much for reading this. I started writing this nearly ten years ago and finally got around to publishing it (some of it I did post on my Linked In profile through the years).

I am 56 years old. I have always wanted to be a writer. I am not saying I am one now – but I have started that journey with this publication.

Don't ever think it is too late to start your dream. Today is as good a day as any to begin.

Remember, Ray Kroc started McDonald's at 52; Julia Child published her first cookbook at 50; Charles Darwin published "On the Origin of the Species" when he was 50.

www.ingramcontent.com/pod-product-compliance
Lightning Source LLC
Chambersburg PA
CBHW070245190526
45169CB00001B/304